ANTONI VAN LEEUWENHOEK

GENIUS DISCOVERER OF MICROSCOPIC LIFE

Lisa Yount

Enslow Publishers, Inc.
40 Industrial Road
Box 398
Berkeley Heights, NJ 07922
USA

http://www.enslow.com

P.W.M. Trap impr.

To all young people who are "curious to know"
about nature, and all those who teach them.

Library of Congress Cataloging-in-Publication Data

Yount, Lisa.
   Antoni van Leeuwenhoek : genius discoverer of microscopic life / Lisa Yount.
      pages cm. — (Genius scientists and their genius ideas)
   "Originally published as Antoni van Leeuwenhoek : first to see microscopic life, revised edition, in 2008"—Title page verso.
   Includes bibliographical references and index.
   ISBN 978-0-7660-6525-3
   1. Leeuwenhoek, Antoni van, 1632-1723—Juvenile literature. 2. Biologists—Netherlands—Biography—Juvenile literature. 3. Microscopes—History—Juvenile literature.
4. Microorganisms—Research—Netherlands—History—Juvenile literature. I. Title.
   QH31.L55Y68 2015
   570.92—dc23
   [B]
                                           2014031244

Future Editions:
Paperback ISBN: 978-0-7660-6526-0
EPUB ISBN: 978-0-7660-6527-7
Single-User PDF ISBN: 978-0-7660-6528-4
Multi-User PDF ISBN: 978-0-7660-6529-1

Printed in the United States of America
102014 Bang Printing, Brainerd, Minn.
10 9 8 7 6 5 4 3 2 1

To Our Readers: We have done our best to make sure all Internet Addresses in this book were active and appropriate when we went to press. However, the author and the publisher have no control over and assume no liability for the material available on those Internet sites or on other Web sites they may link to. Any comments or suggestions can be sent by e-mail to comments@enslow.com or to the address on the back cover.

♻ Enslow Publishers, Inc., is committed to printing our books on recycled paper. The paper in every book contains 10% to 30% post-consumer waste (PCW). The cover board on the outside of each book contains 100% PCW. Our goal is to do our part to help young people and the environment too!

Illustration Credits: Clipart.com: p. 1; Courtesy National Library of Medicine, photo by Jerry Knob, pp. 18, 34, 47 ©Enslow Publishers, Inc., Stephen Delisle, p. 25; Oliver Sun Kim/iStockphoto.com, p. 40

Cover Illustration Credits: Shutterstock.com: ©Marish(lightbulb icon); ©Thinkstock: xrender/iStock(bacteria)

CONTENTS

INTRODUCTION: EXPLORING HIDDEN WORLDS

I n a hospital, a baby lies crying. He is sick, but no one knows why. A nurse takes a sample of his blood. She sends it to a laboratory in another part of the hospital.

A laboratory technician smears a drop of the blood on a glass slide. He puts the slide under a microscope. The microscope makes things look hundreds of times bigger than they really are.

Using the microscope, the technician can see the disk-shaped cells that make the baby's blood red. He can also see many tiny living things among the cells. They are bacteria, the cause of the baby's illness. The technician will report which bacteria he sees to the baby's doctor. Then the doctor can prescribe drugs to kill the harmful germs.

In another part of the city, a husband and wife are unhappy. They want a baby but cannot have one. They do not know what is wrong.

A technician in a different laboratory helps them find out. She, too, uses a microscope. She looks at semen, a fluid from the man's body. In it she sees thousands of wiggling things that look like tiny tadpoles. They are sperm cells.

If the couple is to have a baby, a sperm cell from the man must join with an egg cell from the woman. Using a microscope, the technician can tell whether the man's sperm cells are healthy. If they are not, the man may receive treatments. If the sperm cells are healthy, doctors will turn their attention to the woman. A microscope may be used to examine her egg cells. Either way, the microscope brings the couple closer to their goal.

Many people worldwide have better health because of what is learned through a microscope. This device shows things too small for the eye to see alone. A Dutch man named Antoni van Leeuwenhoek (an-TON-ee van LAY-ven-hook) was the first to describe many such things in nature. (His first name is sometimes spelled *Antony* or *Anton.*) He lived in the country of Holland about three hundred years ago. Holland is now part of the Netherlands.

Leeuwenhoek did not invent the microscope. Another Dutchman, Zacharias Janssen, is thought to have done that around 1595, about eighty-five years before Leeuwenhoek began his work. Still, Leeuwenhoek explored more with this device than anyone else of his time or in the hundred years after he died. He was the first to see red blood cells, bacteria, and sperm cells. Using microscopes he made himself, he revealed an exciting world that few had dreamed existed.

A SELLER OF CLOTH

Some parts of the Dutch city of Delft have changed little in hundreds of years. You can still see the town hall, the Old Church, and the New Church. These stone buildings were already old when Antoni van Leeuwenhoek was born in Delft on October 24, 1632.

In those days, Delft was the third-biggest city in Holland. One visitor described the town as "very clean, well built, and . . . pleasant."[1] Another said it was the prettiest place he saw in the whole country.

Delft is built on a flat plain or meadow. Like much of Holland, it is below sea level. It would be underwater if walls did not keep the sea out.

Canals, bordered by linden and poplar trees, ran through the city (as they still do). The oldest one had been dug around the year 1100. These canals carried as much traffic as Delft's wide streets, and the town was named for them. The Dutch word *delf* or *delft* means "canal."

When Antoni was born, Holland was fighting for its freedom from Spain. Even so, it was a thriving country, famous for its merchants and craftspeople. It controlled much of the trade inside Europe. It had just begun to trade with the Far East as well.

Delft was thriving, too. Trading ships filled its harbor. Its craftspeople made many kinds of goods. Among the most famous were beautiful china dishes. Antoni's father, Philip, made baskets that may have been used to hold such dishes. Delft was also famous for its beer. Antoni's mother, Margaretha, came from a family of beer brewers. Their name was van den Berch.

Learning a Trade

The Leeuwenhoek family lived in a corner house on a small street called Leeuwenport. Their name probably came from this house. *Leeuw* means "lion." (The street's name means "lion gate.") *Hoek* means "corner." So the name meant "the family who lives on the corner of Lion (gate) Street."

Antoni's father died in 1638, when Antoni was just five years old. Philip did not leave his family much money. Margaretha had a hard time taking care of Antoni and his four sisters, Margriete, Geertruyt, Neeltge, and Catharina. (In English they would have been Margie, Gertrude, Nellie, and Catherine.)

Two years after Philip's death, Margaretha married a painter named Jacob Molijn. He had also been married before and had three children of his own. The couple's new home must have been crowded. Perhaps for that reason, Antoni was sent away to school at this time.

The school was at Warmond, a town about twenty miles from Delft. For a while, Antoni probably lived at his teacher's house. Other pupils lived there, too. Later he stayed with an uncle, a law officer in a nearby town.

Antoni's schooling was simple. He learned to read, write, and do some math. He was not taught any foreign languages, though. No one expected him to travel much or go to college. (At a university he would have needed to know Greek and Latin because most textbooks were written in those languages.)

In 1648, Antoni went to Amsterdam to learn a trade. He was sixteen years old. Then, as now, this big city was Holland's capital. It must have been quite a change from quiet Delft.

Antoni worked in a shop that sold cloth, buttons, and other sewing supplies. He seems to have learned the cloth-sellers' trade quickly. One report says that after just six weeks, he passed a mastery exam. Antoni soon became the shop's accountant and cashier. That meant he must have been good at mathematics. It also meant his employer trusted him.

Man of Many Jobs

The big city did not appeal to Antoni van Leeuwenhoek. Delft was his home, and he returned there in 1654 to set up his own cloth store. He married a local woman, Barbara de Mey, on July 29. He may have met her through his work, since her father also sold cloth.

Leeuwenhoek bought a house for himself and his new bride. Houses had names in those days, and Leeuwenhoek called his "The Golden Head." He lived there for the rest of his life.

Leeuwenhoek's store sold wool, linen, and silk to the townspeople of Delft. They could buy ribbons, lace, and buttons there, too. He may have sold some pieces of finished clothing as well.

Leeuwenhoek had to make sure the cloth he sold was of good quality. He used a magnifying glass to do this. The glass made things look only a few times larger than they were, but it was good enough to show whether the threads in the cloth were straight and tightly woven. Perhaps it also stirred Leeuwenhoek's interest in looking at very small objects.

People in places like Delft often did city jobs as well as their regular work. Leeuwenhoek earned some of his money this way. The positions he held showed that he was a respected man.

Leeuwenhoek's first job for the city of Delft was acting as chamberlain for the city's sheriffs. He began this work on January 24, 1660. The sheriffs were the town's chief law officers. They all met in a big room in the town hall. Leeuwenhoek's task was to keep that room clean. In other words, he was a kind of janitor.

When the sheriffs had a meeting, Leeuwenhoek had to light a fire in the fireplace. He made sure the fire was safely put out after the meeting was over. He put out the candles that had lit the room, too. If any unburned coals were left in the fireplace, he could keep and sell them; his job contract said so. The contract also made him promise to "keep to himself whatever he may overhear in the chamber."[2]

Leeuwenhoek did other town jobs as well. In 1669, for instance, he became a surveyor. He had to pass a difficult math test to get this post. His job was to measure plots of land that were going to be sold.

Ten years later, Leeuwenhoek took on the job of wine gauger. He tested the purity of wines sold in Delft and checked the size of the vessels that contained the wine. As both surveyor and wine gauger, Leeuwenhoek had to measure very precisely. That suited him well. He was always a careful observer. He would use measurements a great deal in his science work, too.

Leeuwenhoek's life was quiet, but it was not always happy. He and Barbara Leeuwenhoek had five children, but four died as babies. Many families had such losses in those days. The only child to survive was a daughter, Maria, born in 1656. Leeuwenhoek's mother died in 1664. Two years later, Barbara Leeuwenhoek died as well.

Leeuwenhoek married again on January 25, 1671. His new wife was named Cornelia Swalmius. She came from an educated family. Her father was a minister, and her brother was a doctor. Leeuwenhoek may have learned some science from them. Most likely, though, his thoughts had already turned toward science several years before.

Journey to England

In 1667 or 1668, Leeuwenhoek did something new. He visited another country—England. No one knows just why he went.

As was true all his life, Antoni van Leeuwenhoek was curious about all he saw on this trip. As his boat sailed up the Thames River toward London, for instance, he passed shining cliffs of chalk. Why, he wondered, were the rocks so white?

After Leeuwenhoek landed, he scraped off a bit of the chalk to study more closely. He broke the chalk particles apart. To his surprise, he found they were not white at all. Instead, they were clear or transparent, like glass. When they were all together, though, they somehow looked white.

While in London, Leeuwenhoek most likely stayed with other people in the cloth trade. Like him, they would have been used to peering through magnifying glasses. Like many other Londoners, they were probably talking about a man who had done much more than that.

He was an Englishman named Robert Hooke. He had used a microscope to look at different kinds of cloth. He learned more about the material's structure than cloth merchants had ever seen. He had also looked at mold, cork, and much more.

The microscope showed Hooke things that no one could have imagined. He reported that the cork, for instance, was made of tiny, walled spaces like little boxes. They reminded him of the small, bare rooms, called *cells*, that monks lived in, so he called them cells. This word is still used for the units of which living bodies are made. (Hooke did not actually see living cells in cork, which is made from tree bark. What he observed were the tough walls left after the cells of the tree had died.)

Hooke made drawings and descriptions of what he had seen with his microscope and published them in a book called *Micrographia*. A new printing of *Micrographia* had appeared just before Leeuwenhoek made his visit to England. Leeuwenhoek could not have read it; he read only Dutch. Other people probably told him what the English words said, though, and he could see the drawings for himself. Leeuwenhoek may have decided to start making microscopes after hearing about *Micrographia*.

Soon after Leeuwenhoek returned to Holland, he began going to weekly meetings held by a group of doctors in Delft. In these meetings, one doctor would dissect, or cut up, a body while others watched. The doctors did this to learn more about anatomy, the structure of the body. This subject also interested Leeuwenhoek.

Two doctors at these meetings became Leeuwenhoek's friends. They helped him learn more about science and nature. In 1673, one of them changed his life.

"A Most Ingenious Person"

One doctor who went to the weekly meetings in Delft was named Reinier de Graaf. On April 28, 1673, de Graaf sent a letter to the Royal Society of London. This group of British scientists (although they would not have used that term for themselves, and most did not work at science full time) had been formed eleven years before. Its members met to share their work. Science groups of this kind were becoming popular in Europe.

A Lifetime of Letters

The Royal Society had asked scientists in other parts of Europe to send news of their discoveries. De Graaf was one of many who replied. His letter described "a certain most ingenious [clever] person here, named

Leeuwenhoek."[1] He said Leeuwenhoek was making better microscopes than any that had been seen before.

De Graaf enclosed a letter from Leeuwenhoek. The doctor hoped the society members would like it. De Graaf asked them to write to Leeuwenhoek if they did. Leeuwenhoek, he said, would send more letters if they asked him to.

Leeuwenhoek's letter told about three things he had seen with his microscopes. One was fungus, or mold, such as grows on stale bread. He described tiny cells called spores, which a mold sends out to make new molds. He explained how spores are formed and released. No one had seen single spores before.

Leeuwenhoek also wrote about bees. He described their stingers, eyes, and mouths. His third subject was lice, small insects that live on the skin of people or animals and suck their blood. Robert Hooke also had described molds, bees, and lice in *Micrographia*. Leeuwenhoek corrected three mistakes Hooke had made.

The Royal Society liked Leeuwenhoek's letter and asked him to send more. This was the start of an exchange that would last fifty years. During that time, Leeuwenhoek and the society traded hundreds of letters.

Leeuwenhoek wrote all his letters in Dutch. He used an old-fashioned form of the language. He even

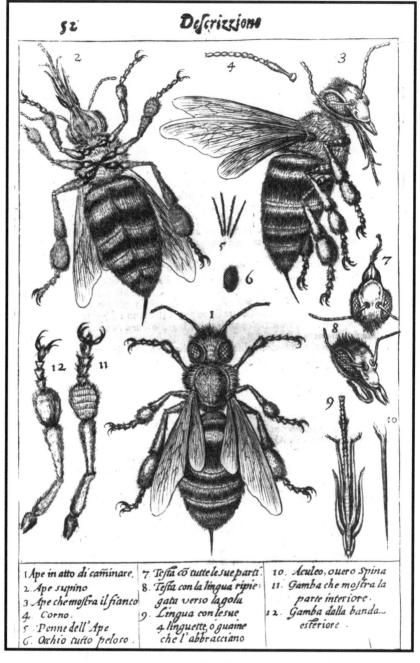

These pictures of bees, made by Francesco Stelluti in 1630, are the first known drawings made using a microscope.

made mistakes in grammar. The Royal Society had to translate his letters into English. (Leeuwenhoek also had to ask friends in Delft to translate the Royal Society's letters to him into Dutch.) Then the group printed them in its journal, *Philosophical Transactions*. Other scientists first learned about Leeuwenhoek by reading these published accounts. Groups of his letters were later published as books, although Leeuwenhoek himself did not do this.

Leeuwenhoek's letters were not like most scientists' papers. They were more like friendly chats. He jumped from subject to subject, often returning to subjects discussed in earlier letters. The letters contained many details of Leeuwenhoek's daily life as well. Each detail told something about how or where an experiment or observation had been made. Such facts can be important in science.

Leeuwenhoek's first reply to the Royal Society was sent on August 15, 1673. In it he admitted his lack of training in writing and science. "I have no style . . . with which to express my thoughts properly," he wrote. "I have . . . been brought up [trained] . . . only to business."[2] He went on to describe his latest discoveries.

Like most of Leeuwenhoek's later letters, this one contained drawings. They showed the parts of bees and lice described in his first letter. He explained that he had not made the drawings himself. He could not draw well, he said. Instead, he asked artists in Delft to look through his microscopes at things he was writing about. They then drew what they saw. Leeuwenhoek checked their work and made them change it if it did not show what he had seen.

Leeuwenhoek also measured almost all the things he described. He was much more careful about this than most other scientists of his day. To be sure, some of his units might seem odd. He compared things to a grain of sand or the eye of a louse, for instance. Later scientists have had to "translate" these measurements into modern terms. They say that a "large grain of sand," for instance, is about 0.85 millimeters (0.03 inch).

Sometimes Leeuwenhoek sent specimens of what he observed along with his letters to the Royal Society. Brian J. Ford, a British scholar who has studied Leeuwenhoek's life and work, found some of these specimens in the Royal Society's files in 1981. The specimens included seeds, parts of plants, insects, and a section of the nerve that leads to the eye. They had been forgotten for more than three hundred years.

A New Invention

In his August 15, 1673, letter, Leeuwenhoek wrote that all his observations and thoughts came from his own work. The same was true of his microscopes. He made each part of them himself.

No one knows just when or how Leeuwenhoek learned to make microscopes. His first letter says, though, that they were "recently invented." He wrote that he had first looked at bees through them "about two years ago."[3] That means he probably started making and using microscopes around 1670 or 1671.

Leeuwenhoek's microscopes were not at all like those used today. For one thing, they were just a few inches long. One could fit in the palm of a person's hand. Also, each had only one lens. A lens is a curved piece of glass or other clear solid that focuses (brings together) rays of light to form an image. In a microscope, a curved lens makes things look larger than they really are. A microscope with only one lens is called a simple microscope. It is really just a powerful form of magnifying glass.

Most microscopes used today are compound microscopes. They have two or more lenses. One lens is in the eyepiece, which is the part people look into. The other is at the bottom of the microscope's tube or barrel. Most modern microscopes have several bottom lenses set in a sort of wheel. The lenses enlarge things by different amounts; the stronger the lens, the bigger things look. A person chooses which lens to use by turning the wheel.

A lens makes things look larger because it is curved. Light moves in straight lines, called rays, but when the light goes from one substance to another, the rays can be bent. If you put a straight stick part way into the water, the stick will seem to bend at the spot where the water meets the air. This is because light rays move through water more slowly than they move through air. The same thing happens when light goes through glass.

A lens that bulges out, like a bubble, is called convex. If it curves in, like a bowl, it is concave. The direction of the curve affects how the lens bends light, and so does the depth of the curve. These things determine whether the lens will make things seen through it look larger or smaller, and by how much. A convex lens makes things look larger.

Lenses must be shaped very carefully. Round pieces of glass are first ground down with sand or other gritty material. Then they are polished smooth with fine-grained putty.

Lenses that make things look just a little larger can help people see better. An English scientist named Roger Bacon pointed this out in the thirteenth century. People put such lenses in frames so they could be worn. These were the first eyeglasses. They were also, in a way, the first simple microscopes.

Late in the sixteenth century, people learned how to make lenses that enlarged things much, much more. Some were used in compound microscopes. No one knows for sure who invented such microscopes, but they were in use more than thirty years before Leeuwenhoek was born.

Why did Leeuwenhoek use simple microscopes instead of compound ones? Simple ones were easier and cheaper to make, for one thing. At that time, they also could be better. Lenses made in Leeuwenhoek's day distorted (changed) the shape and color of things seen through them. The larger and stronger the lens, the worse these problems were. Using two lenses made the distortions greater still. A simple microscope could enlarge things more than a compound one without distorting them.

Outstanding Microscopes

Leeuwenhoek never said just how he made his lenses. All we know is that they were very, very good. They were also very small. Most were the size of a pinhead. Small lenses could be made clearer than large ones. Leeuwenhoek's lenses were also very convex—almost, but not quite, round.

An Irish doctor named Thomas Molyneux (MOL-ee-no) came to see Leeuwenhoek in 1685. Molyneux belonged to the Royal Society, and the group had asked him to study Leeuwenhoek's microscopes. He wrote that the best ones he was allowed to see "do not magnify much . . . more than several [other] glasses [microscopes] I have seen." But, he noted, "they far surpass them all . . . in their extreme clearness."[4]

Some may have magnified more as well. Leeuwenhoek would not show anyone his best microscopes, but Molyneux said Leeuwenhoek told him that "they performed far beyond any that he had shown me."[5] According to Brian Ford, the best of the Leeuwenhoek microscopes still existing today enlarges by 266 times; that is, it makes things look 266 times as big as they really are.

The lens of a Leeuwenhoek microscope was set into a hole between two metal plates. The plates, usually of brass or silver, were joined together with rivets. Leeuwenhoek made his own plates. Sometimes he even purified his own metal from metal-bearing rocks.

Just in front of the lens, a pin stuck out from a platform or stage. This pin held the object to be looked at. A screw attached to the platform moved the pin closer to or farther from the lens. That brought the object into focus so it could be seen clearly. A small wooden handle turned the pin around. In a modern micro-scope, the lenses rather than the object are moved during focusing.

Today, something to be looked at under a micro-scope most often is put on a glass slide. Leeuwenhoek did not have slides. If he wanted to look at a small insect, he just stuck it on the end of the pin. For some-thing larger, he cut a thin slice of it with his shaving razor. (He did this far more precisely than other microscopists of his day.) He glued this slice to a small glass plate or put the slice between two plates. Then he glued the plate or plates to the pin. If he wanted to look at tiny creatures in water, he put the water in a small glass tube and glued the tube to the pin.

Someone using a microscope today would look down through the microscope's barrel. Leeuwenhoek, instead, held his little microscope close to his eye. He looked through the lens to see what was on the pin. In the daytime, he stood near a window so the sun could give him the light he needed. At night, he used the light of a candle.

A German visitor described what looking through a Leeuwenhoek microscope was like. He wrote, "You have to put the side of the microscope, where the lens is, against your forehead. . . . [You] look upwards

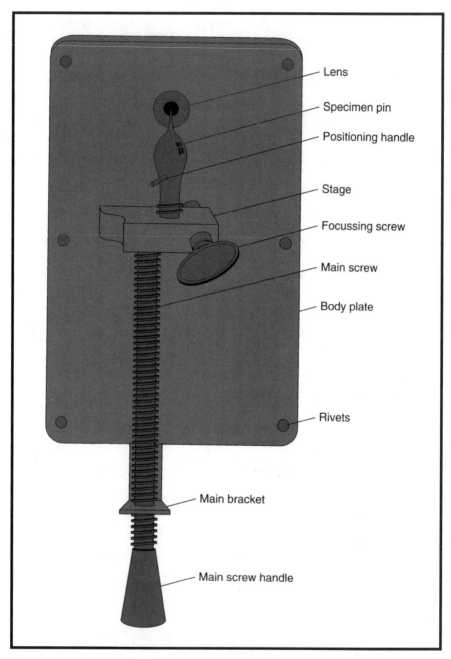

Lens

Specimen pin

Positioning handle

Stage

Focussing screw

Main screw

Body plate

Rivets

Main bracket

Main screw handle

Leeuwenhoek built all his own microscopes. Most of them had a structure like this.

through the tiny glass [lens]. . . . After some time, [this] would become tiresome."[6]

It is easy to take one slide out of a modern microscope and put another in. Leeuwenhoek, though, seldom changed what was on the pin in one of his microscopes. If he wanted to look at something new, he built another microscope. He made at least 247. Of these, Brian Ford says, just nine are left today.

Leeuwenhoek's microscopes were probably better than any others of his time. Still, Martin Folkes, another Royal Society member, knew they were not the real secret of the Dutchman's success. That, Folkes wrote, was due to Leeuwenhoek's "great judgment and experience in . . . using them." It was also due to the time and care Leeuwenhoek spent on each thing he looked at. He studied it over and over. Because of this, he could "form better judgment of the nature of his objects . . . than it can be imagined any other person can do."[7]

"LITTLE ANIMALS"

In the summer of 1674, Leeuwenhoek visited a lake called Berkelse. It was a two-hour journey from Delft. He wrote about his trip in a letter to the Royal Society on September 7.

In the summer, Leeuwenhoek said, the water of Berkelse Lake filled with "little green clouds."[1] Local people thought the clouds were made by dew, but Leeuwenhoek doubted this. To find out for himself what the clouds were made of, he put some of the lake water in a glass tube and looked at it through one of his microscopes.

Leeuwenhoek saw "earthy particles, and some green streaks."[2] Each streak, he wrote, was about as thick as a strand of human hair. The streaks coiled in spirals, like snakes. Far stranger, though, were:

> many . . . animalcules [little animals]. . . . Some were roundish, while others, a bit bigger, consisted of an oval [were egg-shaped]. On these last I saw two little legs near the head and two little fins at the hindmost [rear] end of the body. Others were somewhat longer than an oval, and these were very slow in moving and few in number. These animalcules had divers [different] colors, some being whitish and transparent [clear]; others with green and glittering little scales. . . . The motion of most of these animalcules in the water was so swift, and so various, upwards, downwards, and roundabouts, that it was wonderful to see.[3]

These creatures, Leeuwenhoek said, were about a thousand times smaller than the smallest living thing he had seen so far: a tiny, spiderlike mite that lived on cheese. Cheese mites are smaller than the dot at the end of this sentence.

No one had dreamed that such minute living things existed. They could be seen only through a good microscope. Even Hooke had not found them. Leeuwenhoek would study many kinds of "little animals" during his life. They were his greatest discovery.

Today, many scientists would place most of Leeuwenhoek's "little animals" in a large group of living things called protists. Protists are neither plants nor animals.

Most, though not all, have just one cell. There are many kinds of protists, including some that are helpful to humans, such as the yeasts used to make bread and beer. Algae (sometimes called seaweeds) are also protists. Leeuwenhoek described his "animalcules" so well that modern scientists often can tell which kinds he saw.

Many Kinds of Creatures

Two years after his visit to Berkelse Lake, Leeuwenhoek described living things visible only through a microscope, or microbes, in much more detail. He had looked for them in water from rain, melted snow, and the sea. He had studied drinking water from his well, too. He saw "little animals" in all of these. One of his favorite places to look for them, he wrote, was in water in which black pepper had been soaked. Such water may have revealed microbes that had lived on the pepper grains as well as those already in the water itself.

Leeuwenhoek sent a long letter to the Royal Society about his little animals on October 9, 1676. Part of it was a sort of journal. He told how the numbers and kinds of microbes in water from different sources had changed from day to day.

The first microbes Leeuwenhoek described were in rainwater that had stayed in a pot for several days.

One microbe was a protist now called vorticella. Leeuwenhoek wrote that these creatures "sometimes stuck out two little horns. . . . [These] moved after the fashion of a horse's ears. The part between these little horns was flat, their body else being roundish. . . . It ran somewhat to a point at the hind end. . . . [At this] end it had a tail, near four times as long as the whole body."[4]

Leeuwenhoek called the vorticellae "the most wretched creatures that I have ever seen."[5] He felt sympathy for them because the tails of the vorticellae seemed to catch on things all the time. When this happened, he said, "they pulled their body out into an oval, and did struggle, by strongly stretching themselves, to get their tail loose. . . . Their whole body then sprang back towards the pellet [end] of the tail, and their tails then coiled up serpent-wise. . . . This motion of stretching out and pulling together of the tail continued."[6]

Leeuwenhoek wrote about vorticellae again late in his life. By then he understood the little creatures much better. He most likely had seen them through better microscopes than those he first used. He changed his ideas when his observations gave him new information, an important process in science.

For one thing, Leeuwenhoek had come to realize that tiny, hairlike structures went all around the top of each vorticella's bell-shaped body. These hairs formed a circle. From some angles, the hairs at the ends of the circle looked bunched together. He had thought at first that these bunches were horns, because he had not seen the hairs outside the bunches. He now knew that this circle of hairs stirred up the water, which brought food bits to the animal.

He no longer felt so sorry for the vorticellae. He knew that their tails were not caught by accident. Instead, the animals attached themselves to water plants. They moved up and down to escape danger or catch food.

Leeuwenhoek found some of the most interesting microbes in what he called pepper-water. He had wondered what made pepper taste so hot. He thought bits of pepper might be shaped like tiny needles that pricked the tongue. To find out if this was so, he soaked pepper in water for three weeks. He hoped that doing so would make the large pieces of pepper come apart so he could examine them.

On April 24, 1676, Leeuwenhoek looked at the pepper-water under a microscope. To his surprise, he found four kinds of microbes in it. One kind, he wrote, "were incredibly small. . . . I judged that if a hundred of them. . . . lay stretched out one by another, they would not equal the length of a coarse grain of sand. . . . Ten hundred thousand of them . . . could not equal the dimensions [volume] of a grain of such coarse sand."[7] The only one-celled creatures this small are bacteria. Leeuwenhoek was the first to see them.

"Fairy Tales"?

The Royal Society had trouble believing Leeuwenhoek's reports about the little animals. To convince the doubters, Leeuwenhoek sent the society letters from eight men, including ministers, lawyers, and doctors. The men signed the letters under oath and swore that they had seen the tiny creatures.

The British scientists still wanted to see for themselves. They made their own pepper-water and looked at it under microscopes, but they found no living things. They then asked Robert Hooke to repeat Leeuwenhoek's experiments. By then, Hooke was a chief officer of the society. He had not used microscopes for years.

Late in 1677, Robert Hooke used one of his old microscopes to examine water in which pepper or grain had been soaked. He found "very small creatures swimming up and down" in all his mixtures.[8] Like Leeuwenhoek, he found the greatest variety of

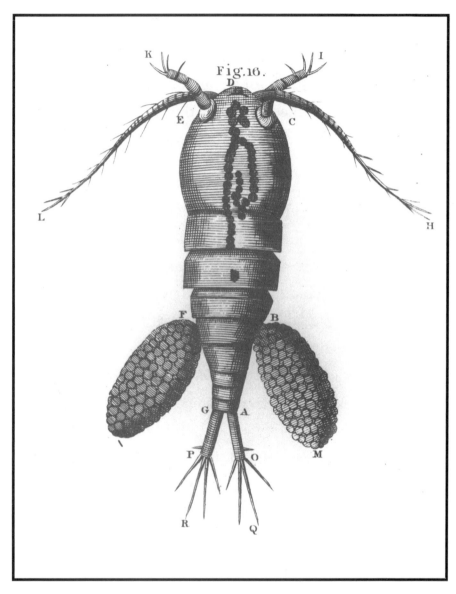

In addition to microbes, Leeuwenhoek studied larger creatures that lived in water, such as this shrimplike animal. It was tiny, but could perhaps be seen with the naked eye.

microbes in pepper-water. Some of these, probably protists, seemed like "gigantic monsters" compared to the many smaller ones (bacteria) that "almost filled the water."[9]

Hooke showed these microscopic creatures to the Royal Society at several of the Society's meetings. On November 15, 1677, a society member named Birch recorded, "There was no longer any doubt of Mr. Leeuwenhoek's discovery."[10]

This was not true outside the society. Over the years, many people questioned this part of Leeuwenhoek's work, including both visiting scientists and neighbors in Delft. Leeuwenhoek grew used to hearing that he told "fairy tales about the little animals."[11] Still, he swore he had seen all he claimed—and more.

How did these microbes get into water? Some thought they were made from nonliving matter, an idea called spontaneous generation, but Leeuwenhoek did not share this belief. He was sure that the tiny creatures had come from parents like themselves. He thought they might be carried on dust that floats in the air. He found that some microbes could live for a long time in dried form. He thought they might be drawn up into the air when water dried up. Then, when it rained, they might be brought back down from the clouds with the rainwater. Now we know that some microbes do move from place to place in this way.

"Little Animals" in the Body

Finding microbes in water was startling enough, but Leeuwenhoek went on to see them in the bodies of people as well. In a letter dated September 17, 1683, he described the "little animals" he found on people's teeth.

He started with his own teeth. He told the Royal Society that he cleaned his teeth daily. This, he knew, was not common. Because he did so, he wrote, "my teeth are . . . clean and white. . . . Few persons of my age [fifty-one] can show so good a set." Still, he could see in a mirror that a "white substance . . . like a mixture of flour and water" stuck to his teeth.[12] He saw it mostly on the back ones. Dentists now call this substance plaque. It is made of food bits, saliva (spit), and bacteria.

Leeuwenhoek guessed that little animals might live in this matter. He scraped some off and mixed it with his saliva to make it thin enough to see through. He then saw "many very small animalcules. . . . The largest sort . . . [was] leaping about in the fluid like the fish called a jack. . . . The second sort . . . had a . . . whirling motion." A third kind were too small for him to make out their shape. They moved like "gnats, or flies, sporting in the air."[13]

He went on to look at scrapings from other people's mouths. He found that people who never cleaned their teeth had the most "little animals." He guessed that these creatures caused such people's "stinking" breath. Even clean mouths, however, held microbes by the millions. "All the people living in our United Netherlands," Leeuwenhoek wrote, "are not as many as the living animals that I carry in my own mouth this very day."[14]

There was nothing Leeuwenhoek would not look at. Once he was sick and had loose bowel movements. He studied those, too! On November 12, 1680, he wrote that he had found little animals there as well. "Their bodies were somewhat longer than broad. . . . Their belly, which was flat-like, . . . [had] little paws. . . . They made . . . a stir in the clear medium [fluid]."[15]

These creatures had probably made Leeuwenhoek sick. Most likely they were a kind of protist called *Giardia*, which lives in the intestine. People still get sick from drinking water with *Giardia* in it.

Leeuwenhoek never seemed to guess, though, that some of his "little animals" might cause illness. This may have been because he found microbes in so many places. They were in the bodies of healthy people and animals. They were in water that people could drink without getting sick. Most of the microbes he saw—indeed, most of the microbes that exist—in fact are harmless to humans. Some are even helpful. Microbes are used in some factory processes, such as tanning leather. Other microbes provide valuable drugs.

In 1693, one visitor claimed that Leeuwenhoek had discovered "more kinds of invisible animals than the world before him knew there were visible ones."[16] This was an exaggeration—but perhaps not by much.

Leeuwenhoek himself was delighted by his "little animals." He wrote that "among all the marvels that I have discovered in nature, [these are] the most marvelous of all."[17] Many modern scientists would agree with him.

Chapter 4

CREEPY-CRAWLIES

A ntoni van Leeuwenhoek's neighbors might
have been shocked to learn what was in his
pockets. Why, they would have wondered,
did he carry around a box of tiny worms?

Studying Insects' Lives

Carrying worms in his pocket helped Leeuwenhoek
study insects, another of the many groups of living
things he examined during his long life. The "worms"
were larvae, the young of certain insects. He had
watched them hatch from eggs. He knew they must
have warmth to stay alive. The only way to keep them
warm in cold Dutch winters, he found, was to put
them next to his body.

Sometimes he even got other family members to help. Once he asked his wife to keep a box of silkworm eggs under her clothes. (Silkworms are the larvae of a kind of moth.) Another time she did the same with a box of mites. She must have been a patient woman!

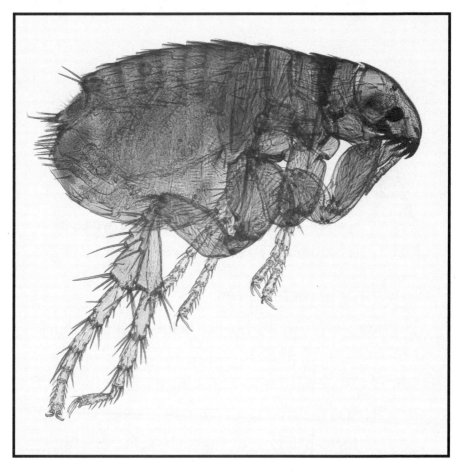

Leeuwenhoek studied adult fleas like this one. He let them bite his hand to get the blood they needed. He also killed flies to feed the larvae.

Leeuwenhoek studied sixty-seven kinds of insects. He also looked at other small living things, such as spiders and shrimp. He watched them grow from eggs to adults. At each stage of their lives, he put them under his microscopes.

He had no trouble finding insects to look at. Ants lived in his backyard. Insect pests showed up in apples from his orchard. When he wanted to study fleas, he just asked the maid to catch some around the house. Tiny mites infested stored food in his kitchen. He had to buy lice, but wrote, "I had plenty of them brought to me for my money."[1]

Carrying larvae or eggs in his pocket was not all Leeuwenhoek went through to study insects. He killed flies to feed to his flea larvae. He put up with stings so he could see inside an ants' nest. (He wrote that the stings "gave me more pain than in my life before I had experienced from them.")[2] He knew that adult fleas and lice had to drink fresh blood, so he let them bite his hands.

Only once were Leeuwenhoek's experiments too much for him. He wanted to learn how many young lice would appear in a certain length of time. He therefore put two female lice into a clean sock and wore it. He used a black sock instead of his usual white one, so that the pale lice and their eggs would show up clearly on the dark cloth. Using strips of another sock, he tied the first one shut at the knee to keep the lice from escaping.

After six days, he found that each female had laid about fifty eggs in the sock. He then put the sock back on, eggs and all, for another ten days. By that time, he found that about twenty-five of the eggs had hatched into young lice. More were ready to hatch.

Leeuwenhoek did not wait for them. He knew he was just "enduring, in one leg, what most poor people . . . suffer in their whole bodies . . . all their lives." Still, he had had enough. As he told the Royal Society, "I was . . . disgusted at the sight of so many lice. . . . I threw the stocking containing them into the street." After that, he "rubbed [his] leg and foot very hard" to kill any lice still there.[3] Then he went back to clean white stockings.

How Insects' Bodies Work

When Leeuwenhoek studied an insect or other creature, he did more than watch it grow up. He carried out experiments to learn how its body worked. He did this with spiders, for instance. Spiders are arachnids, not insects, but they are related to insects.

Most spiders spin webs from silky threads. Leeuwenhoek wanted to know how they made those threads.

He saw that the thread came from the rear of a spider's body. Was there one thread, or several? At first he could not tell.

Leeuwenhoek found a way to glue a spider on its back, so that it could not move the rear part of its body. Then he used a tiny tool, like tweezers, "to draw out from the body, that small part of the thread which projected from the organ . . . from which the threads proceed."[4] This organ is now called a spinneret. He later found that each spider had eight groups of spinnerets. He thought there were more than four hundred spinnerets in all.

Leeuwenhoek learned that each set of spinnerets puts out "a great number of exceeding[ly] small threads."[5] A short distance from the spider's body, these threads twist together to form one or two thicker threads. The strands of a rope are twisted in the same way. The twisting makes the rope strong. Spider silk is also very strong, and Leeuwenhoek guessed that the twisting made it so.

Sometimes Leeuwenhoek would put two or three spiders in the same tube. He saw that small ones tried to get away from large ones. Two of the same size, though, would fight. "Neither would give way. . . . Both of them grappled together furiously with their fangs, till one . . . lay dead," he wrote.[6] He noted that female spiders attacked males, even at mating time.

Leeuwenhoek liked to find out whether common beliefs about animals were true. People knew, for instance, that ants took food into their nests. Most people thought the ants stored the food so they would have enough to eat when winter came. Even the Bible praised ants for working hard and planning ahead. Leeuwenhoek wondered whether this was what the ants were really doing.

To find out, Leeuwenhoek opened up an ant nest in his garden. (That was when he got stung.) He watched the ants store food in the nest. He saw that the food was "for the maggots [ant larvae], . . . who cannot . . . feed themselves."[7] He doubted that the ants needed food in the winter. He knew that some other insects could survive all winter without eating. They went into hibernation, a kind of sleep. He thought ants probably did this, too.

Once a group of Englishmen visited Leeuwenhoek. They mentioned that someone who did not understand something was said to be "blind as a beetle."[8] This saying must have made Leeuwenhoek laugh. He showed the men that a beetle is not blind at all.

A beetle has two large eyes. Each is shaped like half of a ball. Leeuwenhoek showed the men a beetle's eye through a microscope. They could see that the eye was made up of many smaller eyes. Today, the two large eyes are called compound eyes. The smaller eyes are simple eyes. Leeuwenhoek calculated that one beetle had 3,181 simple eyes!

Leeuwenhoek was not afraid to change his mind when his eyes told him his ideas were wrong. He had to do this when he looked at the strange swellings, called galls, that grew on some kinds of trees.

Leeuwenhoek first saw galls on an oak tree. He thought they were the tree's fruit, but he noticed that they grew on the leaves. That was an odd place for fruit to appear. Also, some leaves had several galls, while others had none. Fruit is not arranged this way.

He finally decided that the galls had been made by insects. To check his idea, he cut open some galls. Sure enough, each had a tiny hole in the middle. Inside the hole was "a living white worm, which had very little motion."[9] This worm was an insect larva.

Leeuwenhoek studied galls at different times of the year. He figured out the whole life cycle of the insect that made them. It was a tiny fly. The adult fly laid its eggs on an oak leaf. When the larvae hatched, Leeuwenhoek thought, they bit into the large vessels of the leaf. Water and nutrients oozed out of the leaf. They formed a swelling around each larva. (Almost always he found just one larva in each gall.) The gall held food for the larva. The larva finally changed into an adult, and the adult fly dug its way out of the gall and flew away. In each gall that contained no larva, he often saw the small hole that the escaping fly had left.

Controlling a Pest

Some of Leeuwenhoek's insect studies had practical uses. For instance, he looked at a kind of moth whose larvae ate grain. This moth was a pest. In a letter dated March 7, 1692, he described a way to control it.

Burning sulfur would kill this kind of moth, Leeuwenhoek wrote. He figured out how much would be needed to kill the moths in a granary (grain storehouse) of a certain size. He then tested his plan in a real granary filled with moths. He set the sulfur on fire and then left, shutting the door. He knew the sulfur smoke could poison people as well as moths.

Leeuwenhoek checked the granary two days later. He found that most of the moths were dead, but a few were still alive. That did not mean his treatment was a failure, he said. Part of the problem was that some windows in the granary had been broken. That let a lot of the smoke escape.

Also, some moths had been in their pupa stage while the granary was filled with smoke. This is the stage in which many insects' bodies change from larva to adult form. A hard case most often protects the insects while these changes happen. The cases had saved the moths from the poison.

Because of what he had learned, Leeuwenhoek changed his directions for when the sulfur treatment should begin. He said it should be started as soon as the first moths were seen. This way, the moths would

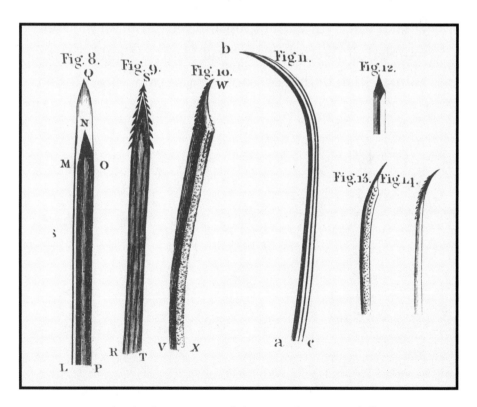

Leeuwenhoek often compared the same feature in different animals. These drawings show the stingers of several kinds of gnats and horseflies.

given no time to lay eggs. It should also be repeated several times so all the moths would be killed.

Leeuwenhoek was glad when helpful ideas came from his studies. They were not the main reason he used his microscopes to look at insects, though. He just wanted to discover the tiny details of nature. Over and over he exclaimed at the beauty of what he saw. He praised the hairs on a fly and the "feathers" (scales) on a gnat's wing. Speaking of a fly, he wrote, "there is a greater cause for admiration and reflection, in the contemplation [study] of so small [and] insignificant an animal, than in that of a horse or an ox."[10]

Chapter 5

INSIDE THE BODY

O ne day, Antoni van Leeuwenhoek picked up a fiercely flapping rooster and wrapped it in a cloth to stop its struggling. Only its head stuck out. He looked as if he were planning a chicken dinner, but in fact he was trying to solve a mystery that had puzzled scientists for fifty years.

Mysteries in the Blood

In 1628, an English scientist named William Harvey had published a book that told how the blood moved through the body. In English, this book's title was *An Anatomical Essay on the Movement of the Heart and Blood in Animals*. However, the book is often referred to by the first few words of its title in Latin, *De Motu Cordis*.

Harvey showed that the heart pumped the blood. It pushed blood out through vessels, or tubes, called arteries. The blood flowed through the lungs to pick up oxygen and drop off waste gas. Blood also flowed through and nourished the rest of the body, bringing oxygen from the lungs to all the body's cells. The blood then went back to the heart in other vessels called veins. In short, the blood moved in circular paths through the body and lungs. Nobody before Willian Harvey had known this.

One puzzle remained, though. Harvey could not see how the blood got from arteries to veins. Marcello Malpighi (mal-PEE-gee), an Italian scientist, solved this mystery in 1660, three years after Harvey's death. Using a microscope, Malpighi saw tiny blood vessels, now called capillaries, in frogs' lungs. They joined arteries to veins, completing the circle that Harvey had described. Harvey had not seen them because he had no microscope.

Harvey's work was well known. Malpighi's work was less well known, and Leeuwenhoek had not heard of it. As far as he knew, the puzzle of blood circulation still had a piece missing. He hoped to find that piece.

Red flaps of skin called wattles hung from the rooster's neck. Leeuwenhoek knew that blood vessels filled the rooster's wattles. Blood showed clearly through the wattles' thin skin, making them red. He put a microscope against the wattles. He hoped he would see the tiny connecting vessels inside.

It did not work. He had no better luck when he studied a rabbit's ear. Leeuwenhoek finally decided that no one could see these blood vessels in land animals. Even at the thinnest parts, their bodies and skins were too thick.

Leeuwenhoek achieved better results with tadpoles, the fishlike larvae of frogs. In a tadpole's tail, he saw that "the blood . . . was conveyed through . . . minute [tiny] vessels from the middle of the tail toward the edge. . . . Each of these vessels had a curve. . . . [It] carried the blood back towards the middle of the tail." The curved part of each vessel joined an artery to a vein. "And thus it appears," Leeuwenhoek wrote, "that an artery and a vein are . . . the same vessel."[1]

Leeuwenhoek also saw capillaries in the tails of small, snakelike fish called eels. An eel's tail fin, he wrote, "looked as if . . . it was composed of nothing but blood vessels."[2] He decided that eels' tails were the best places for people to see blood circulation. He even made a special device for showing this. It was a microscope attached to a tube that held a small eel.

Leeuwenhoek studied blood itself as well as blood movement. He first described blood in a letter sent to the Royal Society on April 7, 1674.

The first blood Leeuwenhoek studied was his own. He pricked his hand with a needle and put the opening of a glass tube against the drop of blood that came out. Some of the blood ran up into the tube. He could then mount the tube on a microscope and look at the blood. Sometimes he spread the blood on a glass plate instead.

Part of the blood, Leeuwenhoek wrote, was a watery fluid. It is now called serum. Floating in this fluid were round particles. He called them globules.

Seen one by one, the blood globules had little color. Several together, though, looked reddish. Leeuwenhoek guessed, rightly, that they were what made blood look red. These globules are known today as red blood cells. They carry oxygen through the body.

As always, Leeuwenhoek tried to measure these tiny objects. He said that one red cell was twenty-five thousand times smaller than a fine grain of sand. That would make it about 0.079 millimeter (0.0031 inch) across. Modern measurements show that he was almost exactly right.

Leeuwenhoek compared blood cells in many kinds of animals. He found that even when the animals were very different in size, their blood cells were not. He wrote that red blood cells were "no larger in a whale than in the smallest fish."[3]

The red blood cells did differ in shape, though. The ones in human blood were round, Leeuwenhoek said. (In fact they are flattened disks, with a rim thicker than their middle.) By contrast, red blood cells in fish and frogs were oval.

Leeuwenhoek also found another difference in fish red cells. He wrote on March 3, 1682, that he saw "a little round body" in some of them.[4] Human red cells did not have these bodies.

The structure Leeuwenhoek saw was the cell's nucleus. Most cells have a nucleus; human red blood cells are among the few that do not. The nucleus acts like the brain of a cell. It controls what the cell does. Leeuwenhoek did not understand what a cell nucleus was, but he was the first person to see and describe it.

Muscle, Bone, and More

Leeuwenhoek also studied animals' eyes. The part he looked at most was the hard, clear part near the front of the eye that looks like a piece of glass or crystal. He called it the crystalline body. It is now called the lens. Like the lenses in microscopes, the eye lens focuses light.

Leeuwenhoek looked mostly at lenses from the eyes of cows. He saw that the lenses were almost, but not quite, round. On April 14, 1684, he wrote that a lens was like "a small globe . . . made up of thin pieces of paper, laid one on another."[5] Each paper-like layer was made of thin strands or fibers that lay side by side in "a very neat arrangement."[6] Every layer was one fiber thick. He guessed that each lens had about two thousand layers.

Leeuwenhoek noted that when the lens is taken from the eye right after death, "no glass exceeds it in transparency." It is so clear, he said, because the layers and fibers are arranged in a very orderly way. This arrangement lets light "go straight through it [the lens]. . . . If this were not the case, the crystalline body would not . . . be transparent but white."[7]

Leeuwenhoek also studied body tissues. A tissue is made of cells that look alike and do the same job. Muscle, nerves, and skin are all types of tissue. Leeuwenhoek looked at all of these.

Muscles make the body move by contracting (squeezing together) and relaxing. If you bend your arm, you can feel the muscles in your upper arm bulge as they contract. Muscles can contract because they are made of fibers that can slide past each other. Under a microscope, some parts of the fibers are dark in color, and some are light. This makes muscle tissue look striped.

Leeuwenhoek looked at cow muscle, perhaps from a piece of beef he could have had for dinner. He noticed the muscle's striped look. He described the stripes as "rings and wrinkles."[8]

He also saw the fibers in muscle. He wrote that the fibers lay side by side, as if woven together. Each fiber, he said, was twenty-five times thinner than a hair. Fifty of them, put side by side, would measure just 1.1 millimeter (0.045 inch).

Muscle fibers, Leeuwenhoek noted, were grouped in bundles. Each bundle was wrapped in a thin membrane (covering). These membranes were attached to a thicker membrane that covered the whole muscle.

Leeuwenhoek looked at muscles in different animals, from whales to fleas. He was the first to describe the muscle fibers of so many animals in such detail. He was also the first to measure them. He found that the muscle fibers in a whale were no bigger than those in a small fish.

Nerves were another tissue Leeuwenhoek studied. He wrote about the nerves of cows and sheep in his last letter to the Royal Society.

Other scientists had claimed that nerves were hollow. They thought nerves were large tubes, like blood vessels. Leeuwenhoek said that there was no hole in the middle of a nerve. A hole appeared when nerve tissue shrank as it dried. A nerve was really made of many small tubes. He thought the tubes carried some kind of liquid. His description is correct, except that nerves do not transport liquid. Instead, they carry electrical signals between the body and the brain.

Bones and teeth also looked as if they were made of small tubes lying next to each other, Leeuwenhoek said. The tubes in bone, he noted, ran lengthwise, while those in teeth ran crosswise. They started from the center of the tooth and went outward. He noticed a hollow channel in the center of each tooth. In living animals, this channel holds blood vessels and nerves.

Leeuwenhoek looked at skin and hair as well. On September 17, 1683, he wrote that the outer part of the skin was covered with scales that looked something like the scales on a fish. He saw that the scales were thicker on some parts of the body than on others. The dead cells on the outer part of the skin do have a scaly look under a microscope. They are not formed in the same way as fish scales, though.

Leeuwenhoek looked at his own hair. He also studied the hair of pigs, sheep, and other animals. He wrote that "hairs are formed with a kind of coat," like the bark on a tree.[9] He saw that a hair has an outer and an inner part. He also saw that a hair is thicker and softer near the root than it is at the tip.

Scientists of Leeuwenhoek's time could not agree about how hairs grew. Some thought they grew mostly at the end, like a sprouting plant. Others said most of the growth took place near the root of the hair. This root is buried in the skin. Studying the hair on his own face, Leeuwenhoek decided that hairs grow from the root. He was right.

Some doctors today study body tissues under a microscope. Changes in tissues can show why a person is sick. A study of healthy tissues shows how the body works. In looking at tissues, these doctors are following in the footsteps of Antoni van Leeuwenhoek.

THE BEGINNINGS OF LIFE

K ill a bull and bury it with just its horns showing. Come back a month later and saw off one of the horns. A swarm of bees will fly out.

Stick a dirty shirt in a bin of wheat. Leave it there three weeks. Mice will grow from the shirt and the wheat.

Most people of Leeuwenhoek's time believed that things like this could happen. They thought that small living things, such as worms and insects, could be made from mud or decaying matter. This belief, called spontaneous generation, went back to ancient times.

Leeuwenhoek strongly disagreed with this belief. He was sure all living things came from parents like themselves. "A flea or a louse," he wrote, "can no more come . . . from . . . dirt than a horse from a dunghill [waste heap]."[1] He was determined to prove that no living thing could be made from nonliving matter. To do so, he worked out each creature's life cycle.

Life Comes from Life

One insect Leeuwenhoek studied in this way was the corn weevil, a kind of beetle. This insect got into places where wheat or corn were stored. It was a pest because it ate the grain. People thought the weevils must be made from the grain. After all, they said, weevils appeared in new granaries. Where did they come from, if not the grain?

The answer to that question, Leeuwenhoek wrote on August 6, 1687, was easy. People brought grain from old granaries to new ones. Weevils were tiny. The people could easily carry them in on their clothes without knowing it. The carts that brought the grain could also hold weevils. So could the grain itself.

To prove that weevils came from weevil parents, Leeuwenhoek had set out to trace their life cycle. Near the end of March, he wrote, he saw some weevils mating. He put them in a container with airholes. He gave them wheat grains for food. In mid-June he saw "two short and thick little maggots" in one container.[2] These were weevil larvae. He cut open some of the adult weevils. He found eggs in the bodies of the females. The larvae must have hatched from eggs like these.

He looked at the wheat grains under a microscope. One seemed to be whole. Still, the microscope showed small holes in it. Inside this grain he found an adult weevil.

In time, Leeuwenhoek watched the weevils' whole life cycle. He found single eggs laid inside grains of wheat. Part of the grain around each egg was broken down to powder. This made food for the larva. After the larvae hatched, he saw them slowly grow into adult weevils. "The beak, horns, and claws appear[ed] by degrees."[3] He wrote, "I trust that these . . . observations will prove that weevils cannot be produced otherwise than by . . . [mating] and laying eggs."[4]

Part of Leeuwenhoek's objection to the belief that living things could be made from nonliving matter was scientific. Each time he looked for eggs and parents, he found them. Another part was religious. He believed God had made all the types of living things long ago. All things now had to be descended from the first ones created by God.

Leeuwenhoek also had seen that all living things were complex. To him, they were beautiful. He just could not believe that such beauty could come from rotting matter. In 1692, for instance, he described a moth. He wrote that it was "provided by nature with the means to propagate its species [reproduce its kind], furnished with eyes exquisitely formed, with horns, with tufts of feathers on its head, with wings covered with . . . multitudes of feathers [scales]." Then he asked, "Can this moth, . . . adorned with so many beauties, be produced from corruption [decay]?"[5] To him, the only possible answer was "No."

Leeuwenhoek learned that not all living things created young in the same way. Indeed, he discovered some ways that no one had seen before. He reported that some one-celled creatures reproduced by splitting in half, for instance.

Tiny Tadpoles

Most living things, though, had two parents. One was a male, the other a female. Scientists of the time disagreed strongly about what each parent gave to the offspring.

People knew that female bodies made eggs. They were less sure what the males did. William Harvey had written that he could not find anything that a male left in a female's body after mating. The male, he thought, must give some spirit or life force that could not be seen. The spirit or life force made the egg start growing into a new living thing.

Harvey did not have a microscope, but Leeuwenhoek did. He used it to look at semen, the thick fluid that comes from a male sex organ during mating. In November 1677, he wrote the Royal Society that semen was full of "little animals," something like the ones he had seen in water.

These "animals" looked like tiny tadpoles, young frogs or toads. "Their bodies were round. [They] were blunt in front and ran to a point behind," Leeuwenhoek wrote. Each had "a thin tail, about five or six times as long as the body. . . . They moved forward owing to the motion of their tails. [It was] like that of a snake or an eel swimming in water."[6] The "tadpoles" that Leeuwenhoek saw in semen were smaller than red blood cells. He thought a million of them would not have the volume of a large grain of sand.

Leeuwenhoek had discovered sperm cells, the male sex cells. These cells bring genetic information from the male to the female. This information helps the young animal develop. So does information in the egg cell, which comes from the female.

Semen is packed with sperm cells, Leeuwenhoek found. He thought there were "more than ten animals in the milt [semen] of a cod [a kind of fish] . . . [for each] human being on the earth's surface."[7] He knew, though, that very few of these would form offspring. In the same way, just a few of a plant's many seeds become new plants.

Leeuwenhoek knew that sperm cells were important. He studied them again and again and wrote about them in 57 of his 280 published letters. He looked at sperm cells from thirty kinds of animals. He found that, like red blood cells, these cells were about the same size in all animals.

Leeuwenhoek's find thrilled him so much that it led him to make a mistake. Harvey could not see sperm, so he had thought that only eggs were important. Leeuwenhoek came to hold the opposite view. He thought all life came from sperm. The female's only job, he said, was to give food and shelter to the sperm as it grew into a new living thing. One reason he made this mistake was that egg cells do not move on their own, but sperm cells do. To Leeuwenhoek, things that did not move did not seem to be alive.

Leeuwenhoek thought all parts of the future offspring were contained in the sperm. Some other scientists soon took this belief a step further by claiming that they could see tiny, manlike figures in human sperm. Leeuwenhoek himself never made this claim. He pointed out that a seed does not look like a tree, even though it will become a tree. In the same way, he said, it was "wrong to assert that the little worms [sperm cells] in the human sperm [semen] are small babies, even though a child is formed from such a small worm."[8]

Some scientists agreed with Leeuwenhoek about the importance of sperm, while others did not. Leeuwenhoek and his old friend Reinier de Graaf often argued about this. De Graaf, like Harvey, thought the egg was more important than sperm in forming offspring. De Graaf agreed that sperm cells were alive, but he did not think they contained a future living thing. He said their job was to bring the matter in the egg to life.

More than a hundred years later, scientists realized that Leeuwenhoek and de Graaf both had half of the truth. Both a sperm cell and an egg cell are needed to form a new life. After mating, one of the male's sperm cells enters an egg cell in the female's body. The result is a combined cell called the fertilized egg. This cell will grow and divide to become the offspring. The body parts of the young animal do not physically appear in either the sperm or the egg. The design of the offspring's body exists in these cells only in the form of information carried in the genes, or DNA.

Chapter 7

"The Great Man of the Century"

The more the royal society saw of Leeuwenhoek's work, the more impressed the group became. Finally, on February 8, 1680, the society made Leeuwenhoek a Fellow, or full member. This meant that they thought he was as good a scientist as any in Europe.

Leeuwenhoek knew this was a great honor. He wrote a letter of thanks to the society. In it he promised "to strive with all my might and main, all my life long, to make myself worthy of this . . . privilege."[1]

Becoming a member of the Royal Society sealed Leeuwenhoek's fame. Later in 1680, a friend named Constantijn Huygens (KON-stan-teen HI-genz) wrote, "Everybody here is still rushing to visit Leeuwenhoek. [They see him] as the great man of the century."[2]

Many Visitors

During the rest of Leeuwenhoek's life, people came from all over Europe to visit him in Delft. Some were scientists, while others were nobles or even royalty. They all wanted to see the wonders revealed by his microscope. For the most part, he made them welcome.

Of the kings and queens who visited Leeuwenhoek, the best known may have been Peter the Great. A tall, handsome man, Peter was the tsar (emperor) of Russia. He wanted to bring European ways to his country, and he was most interested in science.

Peter came to Europe in 1698. One country he visited was Holland. Traveling on the Dutch canals, he stopped at Delft. He asked Leeuwenhoek to come to his boat. Leeuwenhoek seldom left his home, but he did so for Peter. He brought some of his microscopes and specimens with him.

Leeuwenhoek's visit with Peter the Great lasted two hours. He showed Peter and his nobles the blood movement in an eel's tail. Peter said he was "delighted" with this and other sights.[3] Leeuwenhoek may even have given the tsar a microscope or two. (One later turned up in Russia.) This was an honor worthy of an emperor, since Leeuwenhoek almost never gave his microscopes away.

In his later years, Leeuwenhoek was more popular than he would have liked. In 1711, he complained that twenty-six people had come to see him in four days. So many visitors, he said, "made me so tired that I broke out in a sweat."[4]

By this time, Leeuwenhoek lived with only his grown daughter, Maria. Cornelia, his second wife, had died in 1693. Maria never married; she spent her life taking care of her eccentric father and running their home.

Different Opinions

Leeuwenhoek's growing dislike of visitors came from more than tiredness. Certain guests, he felt, had mistreated him. Some had claimed his ideas as their own. Others had made fun of him because of his lack of education. He said criticism did not bother him, but it seems to have made him more reluctant to meet strangers.

Indeed, in spite of his many callers, Leeuwenhoek was rather cut off from other scientists. He worked alone. He could not read the languages in which most scientific papers were written. He thus knew little about what others were doing.

This separation was both a strength and a weakness. On the good side, it meant that Leeuwenhoek was not swayed by what others believed. Sometimes, though, it led him to make mistakes. "Being ignorant of all other men's thoughts, he is wholly trusting to his own," Thomas Molyneux wrote. "Now and then [this] leads him into . . . suggest[ing] very odd accounts of things."[5]

Leeuwenhoek's lack of education sometimes formed a wall of distrust between him and other scientists, especially those who came from universities. When Leeuwenhoek first wrote to the Royal Society, he had apologized for his lack of formal education, but later he became almost proud of it.

He also distrusted students' reasons for entering science. He thought most did so just to gain fame or money. He said they would never work as hard as he had. Worst of all, he felt, they were not "curious to know."[6] Without this love of learning, he felt, they could not be true scientists.

Some scientists, in turn, distrusted Leeuwenhoek. They said he did not really understand what he saw, and in this they were partly right. Scientists are taught to see relationships among facts and ideas. They learn to place things in a framework or system. For the most part, Leeuwenhoek did not do this. He never learned to organize his work. He could not see the things he found out as part of a larger whole.

Many scientists respected Leeuwenhoek, though. In 1716, when Leeuwenhoek was eighty-four years old, the University of Louvain (in what is now Belgium) sent him a silver medal. His portrait was on one side. The other side showed a beehive. Around the hive, bees gathered nectar from flowers. Delft appeared in the background.

Bees were famous for their hard work. In effect, the medal compared Leeuwenhoek to a bee. He gathered facts from nature, it seemed to say, as bees took nectar from flowers. He produced knowledge the way bees made honey. With the medal was a poem that praised Leeuwenhoek and his work.

Leeuwenhoek wrote to thank the university. When he thought of their kind words, he said, "I don't only blush, but my eyes filled with tears too."[7]

Last Days

Leeuwenhoek stayed healthy for most of his long life. His eyes remained sharp. In his later years, though, it hurt him to walk. He also sometimes had stomach problems and trouble breathing.

In 1717, Leeuwenhoek sent the Royal Society what he thought would be his last letter. He was eighty-five by then. "My hands grow weak, and suffer from a little shakiness," he wrote.[8] In fact he lived almost six years longer, and he wrote eighteen more letters to the Royal Society.

Leeuwenhoek continued his studies to the very end of his life. Just a day before he died, he dictated a letter to a director of the Dutch East India Company. The director had sent him some sand and asked whether there was gold in it. Leeuwenhoek reported what he had found. Later still, just a few hours before his death, Leeuwenhoek asked a friend to translate two more letters for the Royal Society.

Leeuwenhoek died on August 26, 1723. By then he was almost ninety-one years old. He died of a lung disease, probably pneumonia. A friend saw him in his last days. He reported that "he continued his course cheerfully to the end of his life along the track of Science."[9]

Leeuwenhoek had seldom given his microscopes away while he was alive. But in his will, he said a set of twenty-six should be sent to the Royal Society. He had planned this gift for a long time. His daughter, Maria, mailed the microscopes along with a sad little note. She signed it "my father's grief-stricken daughter."[10]

On August 31, 1723, Leeuwenhoek was buried at the Old Church at Delft. He had a fine funeral, with coaches, and sixteen men carried his coffin. Most of the people of Delft probably came to say goodbye to their odd but famous neighbor.

Maria had the graves of Leeuwenhoek and his second wife moved to a different part of the church in 1739. (Maria herself was later buried there as well.) She arranged for a monument over the graves that can still be seen. It is a memorial to one of the great minds of science, a man who was always "curious to know."

A MICROSCOPE PIONEER

A friend once told Antoni van Leeuwenhoek, "You've got the truth, but it won't be received [accepted] in your lifetime."[1] In many ways, the friend was right.

Leeuwenhoek knew that most of his neighbors in Delft, and even some scientists, never quite believed that what he saw was real. Late in his life, he wrote: "The ignorant . . . [are] still saying about me that I'm a conjuror [stage magician], and that I show people what [doesn't] exist: but they're to be forgiven, they know no better. . . . I well know there are whole Universities that won't believe there are living creatures in the male seed [semen]: but such things don't worry me, I know I'm in the right."[2]

Most scientists did accept Leeuwenhoek's work. Few, though, really understood it or saw why it was important. Most did not dream, for instance—any more than Leeuwenhoek himself did—that microscopic living things could make people sick.

Advances in Microscopes

Even in Leeuwenhoek's lifetime, scientists lost interest in microscopes. Robert Hooke wrote in 1692 that the Dutchman was almost the only person still working with this tool. Few tried to repeat or add to Leeuwenhoek's work for more than a hundred years. This was mostly because no one else could make microscopes as good as his.

Leeuwenhoek himself was partly to blame for that. He would not show anyone how he made his microscopes. He would not even let people look at his best ones. When asked why he did not teach others, he just grumbled, "I can't see there'd be much use."[3]

In the 1840s, compound microscopes finally became as good as the simple ones Leeuwenhoek had made. Scientists again looked into the world of the very small. Some built on Leeuwenhoek's work, while others rediscovered things he had found.

Nineteenth-century scientists began to find out how cells and tissues worked in the body. They learned that both a male (sperm) and a female (egg) sex cell were needed to produce most kinds of living things. They discovered that some microbes could cause sickness. Others did useful jobs such as breaking down dead matter.

All these discoveries, and many more, grew indirectly from Leeuwenhoek's work. He was the first to describe many of the things that later scientists studied. His detailed, accurate accounts gave them solid ground on which to build.

An Ideal Scientist

Leeuwenhoek's discoveries were not his only gift to science. Just as important was the kind of person he was. In many ways, he was an ideal scientist.

First, he was a careful observer and recorder. He wrote down each detail, no matter how small. The drawings he ordered were just as detailed. He measured each thing he described.

He worked hard and patiently. He looked at the same things again and again. He checked them under different conditions. He prepared them in different ways. He compared the same features in dozens of kinds of animals.

He believed only what he saw. He carefully separated what he had seen from what he thought might be true. If he saw things that disagreed with ideas he had formed, he changed his ideas.

He listened to criticism but was not swayed by it. "'Tis not my intention to stick stubbornly to my opinions," he wrote. "As soon as people urge against them any reasonable objections, . . . I'll give [them] up."[4] He would not change his mind just because people disagreed with him, though.

He was "curious to know" about everything. Microbes, body tissues, and insects were just a few of the things he studied. He also looked at plants, minerals, and much more.

He did his work only because he wanted to learn about nature. "No money could ever have driven me to make [my] discoveries," he wrote. "I'm only working out . . . an impulse that was born in me."[5]

Above all, he loved what he did. "In [my] observations . . . I have spent a lot more time than many people would believe," he wrote. "Yet I made them with pleasure."[6] The beauties of nature made him as thrilled as a child. After describing a shrimp, he wrote, "What hidden wonders [there are] in so contemptible [lowly] an animal!"[7] The best scientists today share not only Leeuwenhoek's care in his work but also his joy.

AFTERWORD: NEW KINDS OF MICROSCOPES

Antoni van Leeuwenhoek's microscopes could make things look larger than any other microscopes of his time—or for more than a century afterward. But microscopes today can magnify objects beyond Leeuwenhoek's wildest dreams. They can even see atoms, the building blocks of matter.

Leeuwenhoek's microscopes used light. So did all other microscopes until the 1930s. Then, inventors in Germany and Canada made a new kind of microscope that used electrons instead. Electrons are one kind of particle found inside atoms. Ernst Ruska, the German engineer who built the first electron microscope, won a share of the Nobel Prize in physics in 1986.

Both electrons and light can be thought of as waves. The length of a wave of light is about 600 nanometers, or 600 billionths of a meter (0.000024 inch). The wavelength of an electron is 100,000 times smaller—just six picometers, or six trillionths of a meter (0.00000000024 inch). Because of this shorter wavelength, it can show much smaller parts of objects.

Leeuwenhoek's best microscopes made objects look several hundred times bigger than they really were. A good light microscope today can make something look almost a thousand times bigger. An electron microscope can make it look 50 million times bigger.

Transmission Electron Microscopes

In transmission electron microscopes, an electron beam passes through a very thin slice of material. The electron beam works much the same way that light did in Leeuwenhoek's microscopes. The first electron microscopes were the transmission kind. With the help of computer software, today's transmission electron microscopes can show the positions of single atoms.

Some scientists study parts of cells with this kind of electron microscope. However, they cannot study living microbes the way Leeuwenhoek did. The cells must be frozen, sliced, and prepared in complex ways before being studied under the electron microscope.

Other scientists look at metals and crystals with transmission electron microscopes. The microscopes can show faults in these materials. Such a fault might cause a pipe break, or keep a computer chip from working right. For this kind of study, some samples are sliced. Others are prepared as thin films.

Scanning Electron Microscopes

Scanning electron microscopes create three-dimensional pictures of an object's surface. They cannot magnify quite as powerfully as a transmission electron microscope. They can show objects down to about one nanometer. However, they can see more of an object at a time. Samples also do not have to be sliced as thin.

In this kind of electron microscope, the electron beam does not go through the object being looked at. Instead, the beam passes over the object's surface in a gridlike pattern. The electrons interact with the surface in a way that sends out more electrons. A detector records the position of this second group of electrons to make the image.

Still another kind of electron microscope is the scanning tunneling microscope. Two Swiss scientists, Heinrich Rohrer and Gerd Binnig, invented it in 1981. They shared the Nobel Prize in physics with Ernst Ruska in 1986.

Like other scanning microscopes, this tunneling kind looks at the surface of an object. Instead of passing a beam over the object, though, it uses a tiny needle, or stylus. The tip of the stylus is a single atom.

The microscope holds the tip just one atom's width away from the atoms in the object. Electrons move, or tunnel, between the tip and the object's surface. As they do so, they send an electrical signal. The movements of the stylus show the pattern of the surface. The computer uses these movements to create a three-dimensional map. The map shows the place of each atom on the object's surface.

Engineers in industry use this kind of microscope to study metals. Some other kinds of scientists use it, too. Some have used it to study DNA, the chemical that carries information that shapes all life. The cells of almost all living things contain DNA.

Electron microscopes take scientists far deeper into the world of the very small than Antoni van Leeuwenhoek could have imagined. Electron microscopes are large and very costly, though. They must be kept in special rooms. Because of this, only universities and big science centers have them. Microscopes that use light, as Leeuwenhoek's did, are much more common. They are still usually the best way to study the kinds of living things that Leeuwenhoek loved so much.

ACTIVITIES

L ike Antoni van Leeuwenhoek, you can do experiments to learn about the world of the very small. You will learn best if you can use a microscope. If you cannot get a microscope, use a magnifying glass.

Do these activities. Then try to answer the questions that follow the activities.

Little Animals

Materials needed:

- jars
- water from different places
- dry grass
- black pepper
- glass slide or other flat, clear surface
- eyedropper
- magnifying glass or microscope
- paper and pencil

Procedure:

Put clean tap water or rainwater in one open jar. In another, put water that has been standing outside for a while. This might come from a pond or stream, or from a ditch or puddle in the street. In a third jar, soak some dry grass in tap water. In a fourth, do the same with black pepper.

Using an eyedropper, take a drop of water from each jar. Put each drop on a different glass slide or other flat, clear surface. Look at the drop through a microscope or the best magnifying glass you can find. Describe or draw what you see.

Leave the jars outside for a week. Then look at a drop of water from each jar again. Do the same after two weeks, and then after three weeks.

Questions:

Do you see anything moving in any of the water drops when you first test them? If so, what does it look like, and how does it move? What changes do you see after one, two, and three weeks? Which jar has the most living things at the end of this time?

Insect Life Cycle
Materials needed:

• insect larvae or eggs	• magnifying glass or microscope
• jar with airholes	• paper and pencil or crayons
• leaves or other food	

Procedure:

Look in your yard or a park for an insect larva. such as a caterpillar or for insect eggs. Other larvae may look like tiny worms. You will probably find larvae and eggs on plants(especially the undersides of leaves).

Ask an adult to punch airholes in a jar lid for you. Put the larva or eggs in a jar with the punched lid. Add a few leaves from the plant where you found the larva or eggs. The leaves will be the insect's food.

Look at the larva or eggs through a magnifying glass or microscope. Describe or draw what you see. Then check again every few days. Try to keep the insect until it grows into an adult. When you have looked at it for the last time, release it outside.

Questions:

How many legs does the larva have? How does it move? What can you see about its eyes and mouth? Does this kind of insect have a pupa stage? How long does the insect take to change into an adult? How is the adult different from the larva?

Animal Muscle

Materials needed:

• animal muscle from uncooked steak, chicken or turkey leg, or lamb shank • sharp knife	• magnifying glass or micro-scope • glass slide or other clear surface • paper and pencil or crayons

Procedure:

Meat is mostly muscle. Working with an adult, cut apart different kinds of meat and look at the muscle. Look for the membranes that divide the muscle into bundles. Look for other kinds of tissue, too. You will probably see bone and fat. You might see skin or blood vessels. Describe or draw what you see.

Spread a little of the muscle on a slide or other glass surface. Make it as thin as you can. Look at it with the magnifying glass or microscope. Describe or draw what you see.

Questions:

How is the muscle attached to the bone? What tissues do you see in the meat besides muscle? What job might each do? What does the muscle tissue itself look like? Can you see fibers in it? Can you see stripes in the fibers?

CHRONOLOGY

1632—Antoni van Leeuwenhoek is born on October 24, in Delft, Holland.

1638—Leeuwenhoek's father dies.

1640—Leeuwenhoek's mother remarries; Leeuwenhoek is sent to school in Warmond.

1648—Leeuwenhoek studies the cloth-selling business in Amsterdam.

1654—Leeuwenhoek returns to Delft and opens a cloth-selling shop. He marries Barbara de Mei and buys a house.

1656—Maria, the only one of Leeuwenhoek's children to reach adulthood, is born.

1660—Leeuwenhoek becomes chamberlain for the sheriffs of Delft.

1666—Barbara Leeuwenhoek dies.

1668—Leeuwenhoek visits England and probably hears about Robert Hooke's *Micrographia*.

1669—Leeuwenhoek becomes a surveyor.

1671—Leeuwenhoek begins making and using microscopes. He marries Cornelia Swalmius.

1673—Leeuwenhoek writes first letters to Royal Society of London.

1674—Leeuwenhoek sees "little animals" (protists) for the first time.

1676—Leeuwenhoek discovers bacteria.

1677—Hooke shows "little animals" to the Royal Society. Leeuwenhoek discovers sperm cells.

1680—Leeuwenhoek is made a Fellow of the Royal Society.

1694—Cornelia Leeuwenhoek dies.

1698—Peter the Great visits Leeuwenhoek.

1711—Leeuwenhoek has twenty-six visitors in four days.

1716—Leeuwenhoek receives medal from the University of Louvain (Belgium).

1723—Leeuwenhoek dies at Delft on August 26.

1739—Maria arranges for a monument to be set up over Leeuwenhoek's grave.

CHAPTER NOTES

Chapter 1. A Seller of Cloth

1. William Montague, 1696, quoted in Clifford Dobell, *Antony van Leeuwenhoek and His "Little Animals"* (New York: Russell and Russell, 1958), p. 25.
2. Ibid., p. 32.

Chapter 2. "A Most Ingenious Person"

1. L. C. Palm, H. A. M. Snelders, eds., *Antoni van Leeuwenhoek, 1632–1723* (Amsterdam: Editions Rodopi, 1982), p. 50.
2. Brian Ford, *Single Lens* (New York: Harper and Row, 1985), p. 28.
3. Brian Ford, *The Leeuwenhoek Legacy* (Bristol and London: Biopress and Farrand Press, 1991), p. 26.
4. Clifford Dobell, *Antony van Leeuwehoek and His "Little Animals"* (New York: Russell and Russell, 1958), p. 58.
5. Ibid.
6. Zacharias Conrad von Uffenbach, quoted in Ford, *The Leeuwenhoek Legacy*, p. 36.
7. A. Schierbeek, *Measuring the Invisible World* (London and New York: Abelard-Schuman, 1959), p. 49.

Chapter 3. "Little Animals"

1. A. Schierbeek, *Measuring the Invisible World* (London and New York: Abelard-Schuman, 1959), p. 58.
2. Ibid.
3. Ibid., p. 59.
4. Ibid., p. 61.

5. Ibid.

6. Ibid.

7. Ibid., p. 65.

8. Clifford Dobell, *Antony van Leeuwenhoek and His "Little Animals"* (New York: Russell and Russell, 1958), p. 183.

9. Ibid.

10. Ibid., p. 186.

11. Ibid., p. 200.

12. Samuel Hoole, trans., *The Select Works of Antony van Leeuwenhoek*, Vol. 1 (first printed 1798; reprint New York: Arno Press, 1977), p. 118.

13. Ibid.

14. Dobell, p. 243.

15. Schierbeek, p. 78.

16. Rev. Jean Cornand de la Crose, quoted in Dobell, p. 62.

17. Schierbeek, p. 66.

Chapter 4. Creepy-Crawlies

1. Samuel Hoole, trans., *The Select Works of Antony van Leeuwenhoek*, Vol. 2 (first printed 1807; reprint New York: Arno Press, 1977), p. 162.

2. Ibid., p. 24.

3. Ibid., pp. 167–168.

4. Samuel Hoole, trans., *The Select Works of Antony van Leeuwenhoek*, Vol. 1 (first printed 1798; reprint New York: Arno Press, 1977), p. 39.

5. Ibid., p. 40.

6. Ibid., pp. 37–38.

7. Hoole, Vol. 2, pp. 22–23.

8. Ibid., p. 65.

9. Hoole, Vol. 1, p. 138.

10. Hoole, Vol. 2, p. 191.

Chapter 5. Inside the Body

1. Samuel Hoole, trans., *The Select Works of Antony van Leeuwenhoek,* Vol. 1 (first printed 1798; reprint New York: Arno Press, 1977), pp. 92–93.

2. Samuel Hoole, trans., *The Select Works of Antony van Leeuwenhoek,* Vol. 2 (first printed 1807; reprint New York: Arno Press, 1977), p. 216.

3. Ibid., p. 238.

4. A. Schierbeek, *Measuring the Invisible World* (London and New York: Abelard-Schuman, 1959), p. 111.

5. Hoole, Vol. 1, p. 231.

6. Schierbeek, p. 127.

7. *The Collected Letters of Antoni van Leeuwenhoek,* Vol. 4 (Amsterdam: Swets and Zeitlinger, 1952), p. 225.

8. Schierbeek, p. 124.

9. Hoole, Vol. 1, p. 274.

Chapter 6. The Beginnings of Life

1. A. Schierbeek, *Measuring the Invisible World* (London and New York: Abelard-Schuman, 1959), p. 196.

2. Samuel Hoole, trans., *The Select Works of Antony van Leeuwenhoek,* Vol. 1 (first printed 1798; reprint New York: Arno Press, 1977), p. 19.

3. Ibid., p. 21.

4. Ibid., p. 23.

5. Ibid., p. 34.

6. Schierbeek, p. 87.

7. *The Collected Letters of Antoni van Leeuwenhoek,* Vol. 3 (Amsterdam: Swets and Zeitlinger, 1948), p. 35.

8. *The Collected Letters of Antoni van Leeuwenhoek*, Vol. 5 (Amsterdam: Swets and Zeitlinger, 1957), p. 209.

Chapter 7. "The Great Man of the Century"

1. Clifford Dobell, *Antony van Leeuwenhoek and His "Little Animals"* (New York: Russell and Russell, 1958), p. 50.
2. Ibid.
3. Ibid., p. 55.
4. Ibid., p. 79.
5. Ibid., p. 58.
6. Ibid., p. 325.
7. Ibid., p. 83.
8. Ibid., p. 87.
9. Ibid., p. 92.
10. Ibid., p. 99.

Chapter 8. A Microscope Pioneer

1. Clifford Dobell, *Antony van Leeuwenhoek and His "Little Animals"* (New York: Russell and Russell, 1958), p. 75.
2. Ibid., p. 76.
3. Ibid., p. 325.
4. Ibid., p. 74.
5. Ibid., p. 89.
6. Ibid., p. 74.
7. Samuel Hoole, trans., *The Select Works of Antony van Leeuwenhoek*, Vol. 2 (first printed 1807; reprint New York: Arno Press, 1977), pp. 274–275.

GLOSSARY

artery—A blood vessel that takes blood away from the heart to the rest of the body.

bacteria—The smallest living things. Each is a single cell with no nucleus. Some cause disease; others are helpful.

capillary—The smallest kind of blood vessel in the body. Capillaries connect the smallest arteries to the smallest veins, completing the circuit that the blood makes through the body.

cell—The unit of which living things are made. Most cells can be seen only through a microscope. A membrane surrounds each cell and separates it from other cells.

compound eye—A large eye made up of many simple eyes. Many insects have compound eyes.

compound microscope—A microscope with more than one lens.

concave—Curving inward, like a bowl.

convex—Bulging or curving outward.

DNA (Deoxyribonucleic acid)—A chemical in cells that carries the information, inherited from parents, that tells the cells how to function.

egg cell—The sex cell of a female animal.

electron—One of several kinds of particles that make up atoms.

electron microscope—A microscope that uses electrons instead of light to form an image of an object.

fertilized egg—The combination of an egg cell and a sperm cell. It divides and grows to become a new living thing.

gall—A swelling on a plant. It often is caused by an insect.

Giardia—A type of protist that can cause intestinal disease.

larva—The wormlike young of many insects; sometimes also called a maggot. A caterpillar is an example. Plural: larvae.

lens—A piece of transparent material, usually curved, that focuses (brings together) rays of light to form a clear image.

louse—A small insect that lives on the skin of people or animals and sucks blood. Plural: lice.

microbe—A living thing so small that it can be seen only with a microscope.

microscope—A device that uses one or more lenses to make objects look much larger than they really are.

nucleus—A central part of most living cells. It controls the cell's activities.

plaque—A thick, white substance that forms on teeth. It is made of food bits, saliva, and bacteria.

protist—A simple kind of living thing that is neither plant nor animal. Most protists can be seen only with a microscope. Unlike bacteria, protists have a nucleus.

pupa—The stage in the lives of some insects between larva and adult. A case usually protects the insect while it is a pupa.

scanning electron microscope—A microscope that uses electrons to form an image of the surface of an object.

scanning tunneling microscope—A microscope that uses a very tiny, sharp needle or stylus to form an image of the surface of an object.

semen—A thick fluid that comes from a male's sex organ during mating. It contains millions of sperm cells.

simple eye—A small eye of simple structure. The compound eye of an insect is made up of thousands of simple eyes.

simple microscope—A microscope that has only one lens.

sperm cell—The sex cell made by a male animal.

spinneret—The body organ, in most spiders and some insects, that makes a silky thread.

stylus—A sharp-pointed object, such as a needle or a pen.

tissue—A group of cells that look alike and do the same job. Muscle and bone are examples.

transmission electron microscope—A microscope that forms images by passing a beam of electrons through a thin slice of an object.

vein—A blood vessel that carries blood from the body back to the heart.

vorticella—A protist, with a bell-shaped body and long tail, that attaches itself to water plants. Plural: vorticellae.

FURTHER READING

de Kruif, Paul. *Microbe Hunters.* Orlando, Florida: Harcourt, 2002. (This science classic chronicles the pioneering bacteriological work of the first scientists to see and learn from the microscopic world.)

Farrell, Jeanette. *Invisible Allies: Microbes That Shape Our Lives.* New York: Farrar, Straus and Giroux, 2005.

Levine, Shar. *The Microscope Book.* New York: Sterling Publishing, 1997.

Marrin, Albert. *Little Monsters: The Creatures that Live on Us and in Us.* New York: Dutton Juvenile, 2011.

Peterson Christine. *The Microscope.* Danbury, CT: Children's Press, 2006.

Rogers, Kirsteen. *The Usborne Complete Book of the Microscope: Internet-Linked.* Usborne Books, 2006.

Stefoff, Rebecca. *Microscopes and Telescopes.* Salt Lake City, Utah: Benchmark Books, 2006.

INDEX